Never before in its history has humanity built a civilization that had at its disposal so many different technologies to accurately monitor, measure and predict its own impending collapse - yet has been so incapable to do anything about it.

CONTENTS

Epigraph

Preface   1

The Plague of Consumption   2

The Dead End of Exponential Growth   8

The Myth of a Sustainable Humanity   15

The Arrogance of Empire   22

The Unhappiness Machine   27

The Paradox of Innovation   38

The Curse of the Self-Destructive Predator   43

The Inexistence of Human Sentience   48

The Entertainment Death Trap   55

The Lie of Clean Energy   59

The Travesty of Government   64

The Fascism of the Human Supremacy Bubble   68

The Fraud of Satan Claus   73

The Illusion of Hope   75

Books By This Author   79

PREFACE

Why is humanity unable to put the brakes on its self-destruction? While much of the world still debates the credibility of such a question, just as the planet's climate and biosphere enter the worst-case scenario of accelerated and irreversible decline, this book takes a no-time-to-waste, unforgiving and brutally pragmatic view. In order to do this, one must achieve escape velocity from the narcissism and speciesism that form the foundation of the "human supremacy bubble" which tints much of human thought. If the author has done anything right, then hopefully much, if not all, of the content here will be listed under hopeless doomism, misanthropy and eco-fascism by those who have been indoctrinated in the bubble. These same individuals are more likely than others to also mistake the book's candid introspection into human history and the human condition as personal insults. This reaction is to be expected.

The space outside of the bubble is cold, dark and lonely, and those who venture outside are already fully aware that they are not here to make friends. They are here to seek truth, and this is often assisted through science, as it is the approach that is more likely than others to rely on facts and events, rather than the evangelical narratives that the bubble has created over the millennia. The essays in this book aim to completely shatter the human supremacy bubble in one, loud blow, by juxtaposing biology with politics, ecology with economics, and physics with ethics. Are you ready?

Bethesda, Maryland, January 2023

THE PLAGUE OF CONSUMPTION

"And on the 8th day of creation, humans took over from God and created capitalism.

And capitalism took over from humans and looked down at them and said: "you are mine now".

And humans looked down at their wallets, and they were full of money.

And they bought everything they could buy, and killed everything in the Garden of Eden, packaged it in plastic and carried it into the supermarket.

And on the 9th day of creation, the supermarket ran out of products. The Earth was scorched, and the oceans were full of dead fish. And humans turned to God, but God was nowhere to be found."

No one knows exactly at which precise point in our history consumption became an ideology. It seems that we always had the propensity to be greedy. However, in the beginning people limited themselves to the essentials - game and nuts which they foraged, or items of special value that they cherished, like a pebble they had found, or a semi-precious stone they had exchanged with an artist from the tribe next door. It was a survival-based consumption, which must also have felt rewarding and satisfying, in sharp contrast to today's shopping which only manages to leave us mentally drained and existentially insecure. Our relationship with shopping today is an extremely complex one: full of self-esteem anxiety, identity issues, social pressure, a toxic cocktail of greed and guilt, and other complex emotions that capitalism has cleverly interwoven into our purchasing decision. After making us feel almost suicidal about the way we look, how much we own, and who we are as a person, capitalism offers us the only way out: "shopping therapy".

The act of acquisition of goods today is a far cry from the time when people simply needed something for their survival and went out to get it. We need to not forget that there was a time in our history when all that we needed was some food and a pretty pebble that we had found in the river. These items were enough, they genuinely felt like more than enough.

Fast forward a few thousand years, and a massive industrial machine churning out consumer products day and night has been set up to cater to our voracious obsession with owning things in order to nurse our deep personal insecurities. When we make a purchase, we are not really buying products. We are buying what these products represent: all the stereotypes, the social status, the personal self-esteem "benefit" associated with each product, however temporary and fake this may be. Consumption has moved from a need-based behaviour to obsession-based, and capitalism has managed to normalize what essentially represents a serious self-destructive mental disorder: obsessive ownership.

The irony is that the more we buy, the less we feel that we own. Rather than owning and making use of the products we acquire, in the end we feel owned and used by these products. They own our mental space, our bank account, our self-esteem and our identity. We have willingly become the personal property of the products we have bought, items that we were supposed to be owning in the first place.

With time, the industrial machine that made all of these products became so highly efficient, so vast, so hungry to sell, that it begun to have a brain of its own: calculating margins, forecasting sales, adjusting bottom lines. It became preoccupied day and night not with serving the humans with its products, but with ensuring that whatever useless crap it produced was sold one way or another, whether people needed it or not. This became the objective of branding: the purpose of branding was to add non-tangible, non-usable, non-needs-based attributes to products in order to make them appear useful.

This was the turning point.

It was the point when consumption became completely reversed: no longer driven by people and their needs i.e. demand, but by the industrial machine's need to sell. Consumption itself had now become a purpose all on its own for the machine, as opposed to a service.

As it established itself, the machine became so hungry for money, so greedy, that it was now desperate to sell anything to anyone, whether it was of good quality or not. In order to sell increasingly inferior products, it had to invent a narrative, a "purpose" that can draw and hypnotize its audience. The purpose was ownership, and the religion that served it was The Church of Consumption, supported by the Apostles of marketing and branding who disseminated its propaganda. The machine itself was God, the marketing campaigns were His sermon, and the products became His blessing. The temples of this new church were the shopping malls, their walls covered end-to-end with millions of adverts of price markdowns.

Consumption was no longer a need; it was part of peoples' existence. The more products people bought, the closer they would get to salvation. Through its power over peoples' minds, the machine, working alongside the Church of Consumption, was now not only owning the people, but effectively consuming them.

Once people had been sufficiently brainwashed, they would buy all of the useless products the machine made. As long as they only realized their mistake after taking their shopping home, the machine had already defrauded them, completed its transaction and turned a profit, with the church receiving a generous cut.

People kept flocking back to the shopping malls, even though they knew they felt even emptier after each visit. They were blinded by their faith. They believed in the new religion unconditionally. They believed that "owning" something is "good", whether it was useful to them or not. The more things they owned, the closer they came to God, to becoming like the machine. And they could brag about their belongings to friends and feel good about themselves.

But they still felt empty inside, because they were not connected to the things that they owned. The products meant nothing to them. They tried to alleviate their emptiness by buying even more products, but all they achieved was falling into further emptiness and debt.

The temples of the new church, the shopping malls, began to overflow with money. The grander they became, the more pilgrims they attracted, the more funds they collected in order to build even more lavish temples. It was a self-perpetuating myth, but long as the new religion managed to reinforce its dogma, the machine saw its transactions multiply and its profits exponentially increase.

As with all religions, after some time the faithful became fanatical. They idealized the machine and couldn't see that it had manipulated them. In their eyes, the machine was perfect. The religion became the biggest one on the planet, merging and engulfing all others under its ideology: Christianity, Islam and all major religions that had at one time preached some level of self-restraint and modesty, were reduced to mere cultural decorations. Consumption, excess, economic growth, became the only powerful dogmas in society, not to ever be challenged by anyone.

Self-restraint became sacrilege. It became an insult to the new church, and to the machine itself. Any concept of conservation of resources was seen as a direct attack on the system, and a threat to the existence of civilization itself. Any drop in consumption or birth rates was seen as an immediate risk to everyone's well-being, even though not too long ago, a settlement of 50-100,000 people would be considered a mega city, usually the capital of an empire.

Society became one big junkie, overdosing on the resources it pillaged from a planet that had been all but depleted. Like with any junkie, there was no measure or stopping point. In a society of junkies, overconsumption became the norm.

The success of our "capitalocracy" lies in corrupting each and every one of us to become complicit in the destruction of the planet, by the time we reach 18 years of age. Accepting the so-called imperfections of "real" society is part of every human being's "coming of age" as they enter adulthood. Legitimized corruption forms much of the bedrock of our social system, and part of the unofficial rulebook of every "democratic" society on Earth. This corrupt civilization can only have one certain fate. Although humans may have invented consumerism, Earth is the only and ultimate consumer. It has an incredible ability to absorb most of the toxic materials humans produce, as well as absorb, recycle and reuse all of human civilization, however it sees fit.

The story of humans did not end well. There was much squabbling over who owns what, and this led to a big war that brought humanity to an abrupt end, before climate change could even demonstrate its ability to do exactly that.

It is estimated that within just 4 million years, and provided humans are completely extinct, biodiversity on the planet may recover fully from the 6th Mass Extinction. Earth can, and will, continue without humans. Humans cannot continue without

Earth.

THE DEAD END OF
EXPONENTIAL GROWTH

Humanity is the weed in the garden that grew stronger, faster, taller than all the other plants, leaving no room for competition. It is the magic bean stalk that climbed so high, it lost touch with the ground. Unable to feel its own roots, unreachable by the bees, it is the poison weed that no one wants to eat, no one has any use for.

It is ironic that the ancient Greek word "oikonomia", which literally translates into "the laws of the house", has a double meaning in modern Greek. Along with "economy", it also means "conservation" if used in a different sentence structure.

The massive irony of this of course is that modern human economies are as far removed from the concept of conservation as they could possibly be. If anything, the key mantra of any economy created by humans is, and will always be, "grow or die" - never "conserve", never "stay the same". The grow or die dilemma is of course false. In fact, the faster you grow and expand, the sooner you die, just like an obesity patient.

There is however one economy in the world who got it right. It neither grows or dies, and actually manages to stay the same, or at least it did, until recently. It is the most ancient economy that has ever existed, and which has been around for billions of years before humans even arrived: the economy of Earth. The real economy of this planet is its forests and its oceans. The currency it uses is water, food, oxygen, sunlight. Its stock market is the ecosystems and climate systems that balance the value and allocation of these resources, and its stakeholders are the 8 million species that live here and contribute to this economy, each of them in their own unique way.

Humans are under the impression that they "invented" the concept of economy. What they have in fact invented is a series of Ponzi scheme economies that tend to parasitize the real natural resource economy of the planet. On the outside, human economies may look vibrant, diversified, and healthy, and they tend to behave like a real economy. There are three criteria however which they do not meet, and which are the giveaways which prove that, as a matter of fact, they are parasites.

The first giveaway is that their balance sheet is constantly negative. Human economies are blood suckers that die once they have killed their host. They are completely dependent on outside nutrients from Nature. They depend on Nature's rains and rivers to water their crops and produce potable water and energy. They depend on Nature's energy, stored as fats, carbohydrates and protein, to survive. Even oil is chemical energy that was carefully captured by billions of plants through photosynthesis and stored in the ground. Humans never generate currency. They steal it.

Human economies have always run a negative balance: their debt towards nature exceeds their GDP by several hundred multiples, and this gap has continued to widen throughout their history. And since greed is the fundamental driving force behind all human economies, all of them are fundamentally unhealthy, just like a gluttonous diabetic who cannot stop eating. They easily falter, succumbing to inflation, deflation, and all sorts of malaises. They often have to cut their own limbs off, go to war and endure starvation, issues which are very rare in the only real economy that ever existed: the natural bio-economy of the planet.

Humanity's parasitic economies always run back to the CBE (Central Bank of Earth) for a bailout: a new rainforest to destroy, a new river to reroute for human consumption, and so on. They always run to the only healthy economy of the planet for funding. Because unlike the dysfunctional human economy, in the real economy of this planet, until very recently there was no price inflation, no economic boom and bust cycles. Except for rare extinction events, the CBE had a solid, steady performance and a positive balance sheet. The value of the trees, the food, the oxygen stayed pretty much the same for millions of years: priceless, yet renewable. It was an immortal economy, built to last until the end of time. It was founded on the concept of sharing and recycling, as opposed to greed and destruction. In the CBE there are no tellers, no bankers, no cash machines. Everyone is expected to use only what they need and bring back what they haven't used. And still, human economies have all made a run on the CBE, taking out personal loans way beyond their means.

The second criterion that human economies fail to meet is the concept of output. They don't actually produce anything. Sure, they produce lots of consumer products for humans, but this is only one of the 8 million species on the planet. Human economies are parasites because they give nothing back to the host that they have infected. All other 8 million species on this planet make contributions to the CBE, and therefore to humans, and take loans from it when they need. Humans however, are of absolutely no use to Earth and its 8 million species. They offer nothing.

Human economies have no sound business principles, since they are based exclusively on theft, exploitation and the permanent depletion of resources. The human economy doesn't actually have any "output" within the bio-economy, yet human businessmen often brag about what they have "achieved", as if it was a difficult feat. It is in fact the easiest feat for any business, for any economic system or individual to become successful by stealing from Earth. All business steals from Earth, and our contemporary economic systems lie upon a foundation of colonialism, slavery and exploitation within even our own species. This is not called success. It is called theft. If Earth's age was compressed into a single year, modern humans don't arrive until approximately 11:36 pm on December 31st. Only a terrorist can do so much damage, in such little time.

The Central Bank of Earth is the sole big lender that props up the bogus human "economy", but it has already declared bankruptcy hundreds of years ago, trying to service the massive debt that humanity has accumulated. The current collapse is essentially a long overdue default against this debt. The CBE will be run down to the ground, down to the bricks and mortars of its foundation until there is nothing left, because nothing and no one can bail it out. Its assets cannot be "leveraged" or "quantitatively eased", these are economic instruments that only human mobsters know how to use. This bank will continue to be depleted, as long as the human economy is following the main principles of capitalism: Exploit. Destroy. Leverage. Accelerate. Monetize. Grow. Inflate. As long as this planet continues to be run as a for-profit business as opposed to a self-regulating, all-inclusive socialist commune of 8 million species, everything that has ever been created on Earth will end up in a car boot sale. Today's predominant global business model can be summed up in nine words: fuck up the Earth, exploit the people, make money.

The third reason why human economies are not economies is that they worship death, in the literal sense of the word. We live in a death cult. For capitalism to function, everything must die and end up in a dumpster, just so that demand can continue, and factories can keep churning out useless products. The human economy has grown based on this model: converting almost everything into a single-use commodity with a finite expiration date. The core growth principle of all human civilizations has been to exhaust, rather than to sustain. Only if products and life-forms become "consumables" can the production machine continue.

Money has been central to this destruction and devaluation of the CBE's existing assets and equities. Earth's assets are systematically turned into "products", price tagged, and placed on a supermarket shelf, their numerical price nowhere close to their real value, which actually goes beyond the concept of money and is eternal: the molecules of these so-called "consumable products" are meant to go on, to be re-incarnated into other useful things into eternity, literally until the end of time. This of course is not taken into consideration when pricing them. In the human economy, everything is de-valued, and placed on the shelf to wait for its death when the expiration date approaches. Earth has already become one big supermarket, and all of us are working at the cash register, until the fire sale is over, and we all call it a day. Everything now has death programmed into it, and we are all made participants of this death cult. We are made to believe that products, once "consumed", become worthless and need to be replaced by "new" products.

Humans think that they have invented the concept of economy, but they have in fact invented the concept of trash. They have invented a death cult.

Of course, an expiration date-based economy can only be a short-lived system. Ever since Earth was hijacked by business, all life forms, including humans, have reached their lowest value on record: all of us have become single-use commodities, just like the products that we buy. Everything is bought, sold, used and then made extinct in Earth's final, closing down sale. If you treat natural resources and people as consumables, then it follows naturally that one day they will be exhausted. If you treat the world as trash, then trash is what it will become.

Nothing was ever meant to be "consumed" on Earth. Everything is eventually recycled, including civilizations. If every time we used the word "consume" in a sentence we instead replaced it with "borrow", which is more accurate, we would perhaps realize the massive debt towards Earth that humanity has amassed, and the predicament that it is in. Go on, try it.

All institutions within these "economies" were therefore built with the aim of supporting, organizing and streamlining the death cult of accelerated growth and natural exhaustion. The unsustainable nature of these institutions means that they will undoubtedly collapse, taking all of civilization down with them. This is a natural process that is impossible to stop, as stopping it would require the radical and complete redesign of the fundamental driving principle behind these institutions, as well as the operation of the societies that support them, both at the individual and collective level. The entirety of humanity has already become one big business, and each of us is, willingly or not, part of this ever-growing, destructive, polluting, utterly pointless corporation. Our civilization has become a monster: destroying our environment and using each and every one of us individually to achieve this goal. As a result, almost all humans on planet Earth have a vested interest in seeing this planet destroyed: whether to keep their jobs or maintain their lifestyle, they are hostage to a system of natural destruction that they can simply never unshackle themselves from.

But the accounting department has no clue how to run things. It is staffed by a bunch of mafia mobsters. In fact, the human economy is a Ponzi scheme, holding the entirety of Earth's economy hostage, and making every single human participant a stakeholder who has everything to lose if it all goes south. These stakeholders then go on to devise the religions, lies and myths that they need to keep telling themselves, and everybody else, in order to keep the Ponzi scheme going.

As with all Ponzi schemes, exponential growth is always followed by exponential collapse. The human garbage party will soon be over, ending in a spectacular plastic bonfire.

"Sorry Humans, my records show that there are no funds left in your account" – Central Bank of Earth

THE MYTH OF A SUSTAINABLE HUMANITY

There was a time when humans were foragers. There were no supermarkets, not even agriculture – in other words, there was no "food production system" as such. The system was Earth itself, and it was the level of food supply that moderated demand, which in turn, controlled population (and this further limited demand). As long as the size of human population was directly linked to this natural supply of food and other resources, we were still a mere link in the food chain, as opposed to a predator of the entire system.

People collected food from their immediate environment: fruit, nuts, animals and fish they could kill. It has been argued that this lifestyle inflicted little damage to the land and to animal populations, allowing the ecosystem to maintain its overall balance and still manage supply and demand. The berry bushes were able to regenerate and make more berries. The fish in the river that weren't caught this year laid their eggs so that humans can have both berries and fish next year, and the year after. We were seemingly in balance with the ecosystem.

Or were we? Because surely if those early foragers had today's human population size of 8 billion, those poor berry bushes and fish in the river would be extinct within a few weeks. Therefore, was it the lifestyle of the foragers that was in balance with the Earth, or was it the fact that their population size, and therefore the level of damage they inflicted, was negligible, allowing Earth to recover each year and produce again?

As it turns out, the more information we uncover about our prehistoric ancestors, the more it becomes apparent that they were almost just as bad as us when it comes to mentality. Whenever and wherever prehistoric humanity expanded geographically, species that were tasty, such as big animals, "mysteriously" disappear from the fossil record at around the same exact time as the arrival of humans.

45,000 years ago, humans invaded the unique ecosystem of Australia, burning down the forest and eventually making 24 of its 25 largest animals extict. Today's Australian Eucalyptus forests may actually be the remnants of the forest that survived the blaze: eucalyptus was the tree that regenerated the fastest and was able to repopulate the charred woodland.

Much of what we consider today to be "wilderness" is actually the meagre remnants of a much richer, much more diverse nature that once existed on this planet: one which we will never be able to see, or even imagine: a world that the first foragers slashed and burned to the ground, pillaged and made extinct, as they moved from foraging to agriculture and onwards to industrial, technological societies.

Rather than living in balance with the natural supply of food, we have been engaged in an aggressive competitive struggle with nature since the beginning of our existence as Homo sapiens. The fact that there were no immediate consequences stemming from our actions on the natural environment, only resulted in arrogance. Our tribes, and later our organized societies, were built on a foundation of natural exploitation that never felt "wrong" in any way. It was accepted as part of our "nature". Our economic and religious structures further emboldened and rubberstamped this perception that our natural role is to exploit and destroy the ecosystem that we are part of. A web of traditions, myths and religions based on human supremacy over other species further quelled any possible doubts and second thoughts on whether what we were doing was wrong. Any potential thoughts of guilt, regret or remorse for natural destruction were simply not part of the conversation, once we had convinced ourselves of our role, and accepted ourselves for what we are.

Once we had functionally, spiritually and fiscally accepted that we were in an exploitation relationship with nature, we had effectively declared war on the planet. An aggressive narrative of "humans vs. nature" permeated all of our advanced civilisations, and further supported the message that we are not part of nature. We are separate from it, and we are better. In order to strengthen this human supremacy narrative and justify the war, nature had to be portrayed as the villain. It was often depicted as dangerous, raw, threatening and an enemy of humanity.

This spiritual separation began to translate into a physical one, as the first human settlements were set up as fortresses against the "wilderness" and "disorder" of nature. An entirely new world was created: the indoor living space, a habitat reserved exclusively for human use, and which represented the antithesis to anything natural. Our front porches became the physical boundaries between the natural and the human world. They became trenches in our new war against nature, and Earth. At the same time, we created outdoor spaces that were reserved exclusively for human exploitation. Large-scale commercial agriculture has been the most devastating human warfare against the planet, using military-style annihilation techniques to wipe out entire ecosystems, down to the microorganisms in the soil. Locusts are far less harmful in comparison.

Of course, this physical and spiritual separation from nature was an illusion. Humans needed to be tangibly near the resources they usurped. All historic human cities have been illegally built on the most water-rich, most biologically diverse habitats: usually a river delta, a fertile valley, or other sheltered location. The species that once inhabited these locations were made extinct by humans such a long time ago that, we don't even know who they were or what they looked like. Whatever is left of these habitats, and all the species that still live in them, are under attack by 8 billion hungry, wasteful water faucets that deplete water out of Earth's remaining ecosystems twenty-four hours a day. While the worst of the climate crisis is only just beginning, the extinction apocalypse has already been largely perpetrated. We have driven to extinction not only countless plants and animals, but other species of intelligent humanoids like us that used to inhabit this planet. We are now simply finishing off whatever is left. The rich biodiversity legacy of this planet has already largely been forgotten. There are many humans who have grown up exclusively in cities and seen nothing but concrete walls and pollution all their lives. They are ignorant of what nature is, and that protecting it is critical to the continuation of their own species. If we have truly disconnected ourselves this much from the ecosystem that feeds us, we might as well be pronounced technically dead.

The myths about primitive tribes of humans living sustainably in harmony with nature aim to pave over our collective guilt, by claiming that humans were, and still are, genuinely "good" at heart but have been corrupted by capitalism. But this is yet another artificial narrative created by our system, much like modern day Germans blaming Hitler for the holocaust. We all voted capitalism into power, just like the Germans voted for Hitler.

Our impact on the planet is not simply a result of "capitalism" and the evil "oligarchs". We are the ones who buy all the products that the oligarchs produce. Humanity's impact on the planet's climate is a mathematical function that represents the summation of all of our activities, and these activities also include uncontrolled, and unnatural procreation. Economic growth brings about population growth and vice versa, creating a positive feedback loop that has locked emissions and ecological decimation into a permanent exponential death spiral. This is the story of our industrial civilization. Population is the big multiplier in this equation; it is the part of the equation that makes our impact irreversible, and our planet irrecoverable.

In the case of the seemingly benign primitive humans, their impact was still significant on a per person basis, especially when it came to the extinction of species. In fact, if all 8 billion humans of today suddenly became foragers, their impact would potentially be even greater than that of modern humans. They would need so many millions of acres of virgin woodland and savanna full of berries and animals to kill, that Earth would not be able to sustain them. Many of them would die in the first round of feeding, while wars would break out between tribes over the control of territories containing the richest food resources.

Most of the rest would die soon after, as the plants and animals that they consumed went extinct, ushering in a food crisis. In the absence of agriculture, and intensive agriculture that is, the population decline would be nothing short of a collapse. Had our technological evolution not taken place, but our population somehow exploded to today's 8 billion, the impact on the planet of 8 billion "sustainable humans" might have been similarly devastating to that of the industrial revolution. The one difference would be that in the case of 8 billion primitives on the planet, we may not have a climate crisis, but only the ecological crisis. Though one can make the argument that the amount of primitive barbeques lighting up every night on Earth across a population of 8 billion may actually push emissions up, over time. I leave this calculation to a mathematician. What IS simple math however is that it really doesn't matter how much we reduce our "per capita impact" on Earth. Our total impact on the planet will continue to be far beyond what the planet can sustain without its biotic and climate systems collapsing, if our population stays at the current level.

We live under the delusion that our modern food production systems have eliminated all risks to our food security. But in fact, we still depend on the both the climate system and animals such as bees, for this food production system to function. 1 out of 3 mouthfuls of our food, 90% of wild plants and 75% of global crops depend on insect pollination. We may read headlines about wars and supply chain issues affecting our food, but it is the rapidly disappearing insect kingdom and the also rapidly disappearing stable weather required for agriculture that are vanishing in the background. Humans only undertake part of the work in this otherwise "modern" food production system. The weather and the insects do most of the heavy lifting.

One of the biggest illusions that many in the environmental movement still hold is that humans were once a sustainable species. It is an argument that doesn't stand its ground from a biological perspective. Our brain has barely changed since then. We are the same species, biologically: with the same anxieties, the same need to hoard, to compete for resources. We may have new technologies to achieve our goals, but the goals themselves have not changed.

The myth of primitive humans living in peaceful harmony with Earth, singing songs to the stars before falling asleep in front of the fire needs to end. Yes, primitive humans did have a higher appreciation for Earth. They did have more gratitude and respect for the power and abundance of nature. They did reuse and recycle more than us. But they, like the humans of today, assumed that this abundance was limitless, infinite, inexhaustible, in the same way that today's humans walk through the supermarket and think that all these foods will be continuously replenished by themselves, until the end of time.

People are still foragers at heart - only that rather than walking through a forest, they have bulldozed the forest to build supermarket shelves to walk through instead. The food in these supermarkets arrives on trucks, ships and transcontinental flights. By the time it reaches our stomach people have been exploited, animals have choked on the plastic packaging, and an entire planet has seen its climate change. As long as the Earth destruction machine is wired deep into the fabric of our society, culture, economy and salaries, we are all criminal accomplices in the ongoing decimation of Earth.

Only when all of us are much poorer, some even starving, will we look back and realise that what we considered a normal, entitled existence, was in fact a life of normalised excess. The tragedy of the human species, and ironically, the ultimate reason for its eventual demise, is that it just never knew how to be mediocre. It never knew how to pace itself, stop and smell the roses, or the disturbing funk of extinction it left behind every single time. It is a species that has simply forgotten how to just "be", and be happy simply by virtue of existing.

THE ARROGANCE OF EMPIRE

A spark, a hiccup. That's all that humanity ever was on the planet's geological timescale. A brilliant colorful flicker, a burnt fuse, then time carries on.

As they grow and expand, all civilizations are easily deceived by their own momentum. After reaching a certain size, they become arrogant enough to call themselves "empires". A web of narratives is woven to reassure citizens that the all-powerful empire will never fail, despite history repeatedly dictating otherwise. The rise and fall of an empire is as predictable a lifecycle as the lighting of a match. Unavoidably at some point, it runs out of fuel.

Whatever the century, all previous empires grew in pretty much the same way: by aggressively engulfing resources and closest neighbors, much like an amoeba. While they may be powerful for a short while during this growth period, for the better part of their lifecycle empires are sustained mostly through terrorism and propaganda, as long as this propaganda is enough to stir enough fear into their colonies to prevent any revolt. The empire gradually becomes complacent, arrogant and impossibly bureaucratic. It is at this point that it enters a period of decline, but it doesn't know it yet.

It never does. Its vision is impaired by the most devastating of ocular diseases: optimism. The onset of blindness is immediate: a "bull" market, a superficial sentiment, a hope bubble filled with blood that can burst any minute now. The fairy tales manage to maintain calm throughout the empire for the time being: the economy will expand, the population will expand, the country will be bigger, better, stronger. We will go to outer space. The more the empire grows, the blinder it becomes. The more signs of an end appear on the horizon, the more the cognitive dissonance becomes part of the culture. This is how all empires live their last days: in denial.

Every single one of our previous empires failed to recognize that it takes an ever-increasing amount of effort, and an incredible amount of luck, to sustain a complex civilization for more than a fixed length of time. Civilizations grow blindly into the immediate space that surrounds them, much like amoebas. They never really "know" what they are expanding into, and what awaits them beyond their immediate borders. They just grow, and then suddenly one day, they don't.

The more complex a civilization, the more difficult it is to sustain daily, in much the same way that the more complex an organism is, the more needs it has compared to a monocellular life form. A human has hundreds more ways to die compared to a bacterium. If any one of our organs stops functioning, we quickly reach a near-death situation. Therefore, when an ecosystem is under stress, it is the complex organisms and predators higher up the food chain who face the biggest long-term existential risk.

All empires are doomed once they have reached a level of complexity that is unsustainable. With their delicate supply chains, political volatility, dense urban populations susceptible to pandemics, complicated food and water supplies that come from far away, mature civilizations may look invincible, but are extremely easy to destabilize if just one of their vital life support functions suddenly fails, as countless historical examples have demonstrated.

Empires usually delay their demise by engulfing other smaller civilizations, parasitizing foreign food, natural, financial and human resources. They set up empire-wide taxation systems, slave trades and so on, so that they can desperately cling onto life by relying on the growth and work of others. They have an arrogant, lazy, voracious wealthy upper class to feed by now, and these classes become the slave masters. Where there are natural resources, there will be capitalism. Where there is capitalism, there will be slavery. Where there is slavery, there will be empires.

But as soon as serious problems emerge somewhere in this food chain of taxation, exploitation, bullying and slavery, a chain reaction is set in motion which can bring down the entire apparatus pretty quickly. Clinging to its myths and mantras, the empire is unable to wake up, but it has also become too big to maneuvre itself out of the storm. There are just too many vested interests by now, too many fat cats who will do anything to hold on to their seats, even as the ship sinks.

It is not the collapse of empires that should be either worrying or surprising. It is the fact that they rose to power through the collapse of nature and the collapse of the human. As long as the world order is dictated by economic interest, the empire will always follow the lifecycle of a freshly lit match. The world's existential issues will always be brushed away by elites who would rather sacrifice the empire than step down, much like CEOs of a dying corporation would rather take the golden parachute option than re-draw the company organizational chart. The so-called "elites" would prefer that it all goes down as long as they can hold on to their positions, rather than level with the people and build a world without privilege: a world that they know very well they wouldn't be a part of. Any proposals that challenge our failed socioeconomic system will always be met by fierce resistance by those who hold the most power and vested interest.

This is why the oligarchy that runs this planet will try to keep its wine freezer stocked and will aim to party till the end, even as the climate crisis accelerates and people die. They will try to hide behind greenwashed campaigns that aim to airbrush their image as thoughtful, compassionate, benevolent and progressive "leaders" rather than the selfish privileged slave masters they really are. When the kings and queens of this world manage to convince you that they are "servants to their country", then you begin to understand how clever marketing and propaganda works.

Collapse does not discriminate between rich and poor. When the entire system goes down, the poor may die first, but the rich follow soon, killed by their own guardsmen while drinking their last reserves of champagne. But collapse will always be surprising, even to those who expect it and prepare for it. The latter, ironically, are always the most surprised. But even on the other end of the scale, "collapsitarians" and "doomers" can maintain a naïve and normalized impression of collapse, as they try to come to terms with it. The truth is that collapse will always involve the element of exponential surprise, THAT precisely which you cannot come to terms with. You never have enough time to. It is here already.

So, the end of empires always involves a surprise factor, a denial issue, and of course division, which has accompanied us throughout our history. In a wildflower meadow, hundreds of different species coexist within a crowded space. In a human city, members of the same species are embraced in toxic power relationships, competing like weeds.

As the empire comes to an end, the cost of all resources, services and basic goods skyrockets, just as the value of human life itself plummets, resulting in war. Whichever way one looks at it, war will always be part of the biology of every species. But complete annihilation is an ability that only humans possess.

But please, at least let's keep the show going just for a little while longer. Self-deception and nationalistic arrogance were always key ingredients in keeping the fairy tales and myths going, for any civilization. As long as the patrons in the restaurant have no idea that there is a fire back in the kitchen, they can continue eating their last meal. As long as the house of cards grows taller, it doesn't matter that it is beginning to wobble in the breeze. It all looks good right now, right at this minute. And then suddenly, it doesn't. Denying the truth only delays and enlarges the avalanche of karma that has been accumulating high up above. For a very brief moment the mirror breaks, and all becomes clear. But it's already too late. Human civilisation is a shooting star. Ooops, you've just missed it

THE UNHAPPINESS MACHINE

People used to be genuinely happy, whether they were suffering or not. Unhappiness, in its present form, didn't come into existence until our recent history. The modern version of unhappiness was invented by those in power, whether religious or political leaders. Once these leaders discovered that unhappy, scared people are much easier to manipulate, they began to use fearmongering and "artificially created" discontent as powerful weapons in their campaigns. They used these weapons to distract, confuse, manipulate, and enlist people into their agendas. Those leaders who created, and then harnessed discontent, became the most successful. Unhappiness became a vital element of functioning society. It became a resource, one to be monetized and weaponized.

Unhappiness was a rough diamond at first, but soon these various leaders learned how to extract it, cut it, and shape it into different types of unhappiness that suited almost every single type of human being. Now everyone could be unhappy: however rich or poor, healthy, or ill. The finished product of unhappiness became shiny, mesmerizing, and irresistible to all humans. Thanks to this evolution, today there are millions of ways in which a human being can be unhappy. Just turn the TV on for 5 minutes and start counting the number of things or products you saw which are missing from your current life. You'll probably count at least 30.

The invention, amplification, and monetization of unhappiness eventually became one of the founding principles of modern capitalism. Unhappiness became the most crucial industry on the planet. It became the Unhappiness Machine, ensuring that people are constantly feeling unfulfilled, lost, searching for "meaning". Unhappy people are very useful to society because they buy more stuff. They also tend to buy the wrong stuff and are also more easily manipulated. Ask any marketer, politician, or religious leader. All three of them do the same job anyway, which is sales. The evolution of modern unhappiness has been vital to the development of our economic, religious, and political systems.

The way that the Unhappiness Machine has always functioned is to convince people that something is wrong, something which is making them unhappy, and to offer "solutions" that can alleviate this unhappiness. These so-called "solutions" are often the very agendas of economic oligarchs: "We know that you are unhappy and worried about water availability, so we will divert the Colorado river" (and our infrastructure investors can get rich while nature suffers). Often a specific person or nation is blamed for people's unhappiness, therefore justifying war or other "solutions": "We will invade country X so that you feel safer" (and our defense industry can profit). Whatever the cause of unhappiness, the motives behind exploiting it are always economic. The unhappiness machine is an economic machine, able to enrich the oligarchs that depend on disaster capitalism, empower the religious leaders who concentrate their powers in times of "crisis", and provide the political leaders who were crippled by the democratic process with a carte blanche to shift into fascism.

It is no wonder then, that today people are the most unhappy that they have ever been. This is an indication that our capitalist system of unhappiness is working according to plan. Hollywood movies make us unhappy about the lifestyle that we don't have, which stimulates the important real estate and automotive industries. Women are made to feel ugly and old, which stimulates the massive cosmetics and IVF industries. Our city lifestyle is so brutal to our soul, that we must take long trips abroad to recover mentally and physically, which stimulates the aerospace and hospitality industries. All economic activity is based on maintaining high levels of unhappiness throughout society.

Unhappiness is vital to our civilization. The more, the better. Unhappiness is money. Any good marketer knows this. Our economic and political systems depend on keeping us unhappy and unfulfilled, so that they can continue to control us and sell us "things" and ideas. Most things that humans "need" today are not actual needs. They are implanted fantasies, obsessions, and insecurities.

Without existential unhappiness, neither capitalism or fascism would survive. Our leaders depend on us feeling unhappy and scared, so that they can manipulate and distract us from the issues that they know they cannot solve (or do not want to solve). Their ultimate goal? Absolutely none, they have no goals. They don't even have these "hidden agendas" everyone is talking about in their conspiracy theories. All they care about is simply maintaining their position, the current power structures, and existing religious and economic institutions that support them.

These structures are so efficiently integrated into the Unhappiness Machine that they almost maintain themselves: they have evolved over thousands of years of human civilization with the sole purpose of perpetuating and monetizing unhappiness. They have stood the test of time because they run on fear, the most timeless of emotions. They run on humans who are first and foremost scared consumers: running around all day shopping to temporarily cure their insecurities, carefully implanted by marketing messages.

But they also run on our fear of death and trauma. We are all born into a system that exploits us and traumatizes us, every single day. The human being is the most traumatized animal on Earth. Humans are so conditioned to their own trauma that they cannot feel it anymore: it has become part of their identity, so much so that they confuse feeling trauma with feeling alive. They actively seek it, in all forms of self-destructive addictions such as drugs and consumption, hoping that they will revisit it and numb the pain, while in the meantime they make sure to inflict trauma on all other 8 million species of this planet, to falsely affirm their supremacy over trauma, pain, fear, and death.

Capitalism's manipulative genius was in that it managed to turn people against themselves, without them even realizing just how, and when, they had been manipulated and traumatized. Capitalism's marketing techniques made people feel so empty, inadequate, and insecure about themselves, that selling them anything was a piece of cake. No one ever dragged consumers by force into shops, forcing them to spend their money. We all became willing participants, without ever realizing that we were accomplices to our own slavery. In fact, very few people today can see just how much they have been exploited. Consumption has become a natural state for humanity, a bodily function, much like eating and breathing. We simply cannot imagine ourselves without consuming for consuming's sake. "To be" is to consume, and to consume is to be. Most of us draw our sense of existence from the transactional act of consumption of products, media, and manufactured entertainment, rather that genuine, meaningful real-life experiences. Those of us who have tried to stop consuming non-essential products very soon begin to experience strange feelings of "non-existing", almost like dying inside, within just a few days into our "fast".

This sinking feeling of "existential death" is of course much like that of a drug addict's withdrawal symptoms: the addict doesn't just feel physically sick. Without the drugs, they feel that they are "not themselves" anymore, that their life has "no meaning". Like any Class A drug that hijacks parts of our personality and identity, capitalism renders us dependent on a lifestyle where we are completely hostage to products and to money for any sense of self-worth. Capitalism is a thief, cleverly stealing happiness and meaning from our lives, so that it can sell it back to us in the form of premium-priced, temporary substitutes of happiness called "products". These of course never make us truly happy, but luckily new versions of these products soon emerge, and the Unhappiness Machine thus perpetuates itself. It is a machine which simply feeds on peoples' misfortune. The more misfortune it creates, the more it profits, getting stronger and smarter in making people feel unfulfilled. Capitalism thrives in the most abundant, yet ironically the most unhappy societies.

All of this was done under the cover of night. Capitalism invaded our homes under the pretense of being the family psychotherapist, but a bad one at that: doing everything in its power to first convince us that we all had some type of childhood trauma or other unresolved issue which needed to be cured. It then pretended to be our benevolent guardian, showering us with gifts like a negligent parent to a teenager who needs real love, not "stuff": "yes darling, you have been through so much. Yes, you deserve this blow dryer with five different speeds. Yes, you deserve this boob job". Capitalism quickly managed to replace our emotional needs with product needs. And to transform our existential unhappiness into narcissism, creating the perfect consumer: self-centered, greedy, and utterly lost.

And what is for sure is that narcissism is much stronger than intelligence. Narcissism can override all other brain functions. Our economic system wants us to be as narcissistic and selfish as we possibly can be, so that we continue to blindly consume without any second thinking of the ecological and other ramifications of our choices. The greatest irony behind narcissism is that it is ultimately self-destructive. An ultra-narcissistic humanity will be busy taking its "selfie" before the collapse of modern civilisation, rather than acting on its predicament. The climate crisis is now the boring drama movie on Netflix that no one wants to watch. Until they suddenly realise: they're the main character in it. As the annihilation of nature approaches its completion, the few lucky survivors will live their last days indoors surrounded by holographic metaverses of virtual, digital happiness assisted by anti-depressants. The end of civilisation will be televised, curated and recorded into the hardware of this virtual un-reality.

Feeding our narcissism further, the world of business and its marketing machine are always trying their best to convince us that they care about us, and that they know us. They care about human rights. About the environment. About the planet. Corporations today are quick to embrace gay and transgender rights, black lives matter and other human "points of difference", mounting expensive corporate responsibility campaigns. These of course are not genuine. Corporations pretend to support human rights not because they care, but because they want to turn human rights issues into "handicaps" that they can monetize. Each handicap is a monetizable source of unhappiness. Each new handicap or social issue is a brand-new consumer segment. The more handicaps, the more unhappiness, the more consumer segments, the more money to be made. There are more useless products than ever which help people "find their identity", celebrate their difference as a segment, and regain their "happiness". Brands and businesses are trying to appear "human" to us, while somewhere in an Asian sweatshop or Brazilian rainforest a human being, animal or plant is paying the price so that the architects of greenwashing and "human rights" PR campaigns can get paid. Corporate responsibility PR has a heavy carbon footprint, but a bloody human rights footprint as well.

In fact, corporate responsibility as a term is an oxymoron. Business never follows ethics or ideals. Business is the enemy of ethics, simply because the environment and human rights are, and will always be, a threat to the bottom line of any business. Business and the Unhappiness Machine thrive on unhappiness and inequality. Business can only be positively transformed when its interests and its bottom line are directly attacked.

Despite itself having no emotions or ethics, capitalism has cleverly taken control of people's emotional world. In fact, it has hijacked our emotions and is now telling us when and what to feel, and how to express our feelings. It has made us incapable of spontaneously saying "I love you" without reaching for our wallet to buy a valentine's present or a plastic toy for our children. Our "love" is so monetized today, that it is breaking Earth's heart. Our love comes with its very own carbon, human and animal rights footprint. A web of capitalist techno-dystopia has come between us and our fellow humans. People used to need each other and help each other. Now they are helped by apps, supermarkets and credit cards. Our own feelings, the most personal, intimate and sincere part of ourselves, is filtered through digital algorithms and consumer transactions before it reaches the other person.

People have become busy consumers: too distracted by their own "implanted unhappiness" to demand a happier life from their leaders, and to even know what genuine happiness is. Modern humans complain that they have no free time, yet they succumb to each and every distraction that capitalism throws at them, which is responsible for consuming their time. They have no idea that they've been manipulated, nor do they know what happiness is, so they keep on feeding the Unhappiness Machine. They have become willing slaves.

Slaves will never run away if you manage to convince them that they are nothing without their slave master. Likewise, consumers will never wean themselves off products if you convince them that their lives mean nothing without these products. They are addicted, dependent, and powerless.

In much the same way as slavery, capitalism has gotten us completely addicted to the products, services, and entertainment distractions that we are willing to sacrifice everything for: our time, our dignity, and even each other. We are the slaves that are in fact owned by these products, services, and distractions. The products, as funny as this may sound, are our real slave masters.

Each purchase is another vote for the system that maintains our unhappiness. Every time we purchase a product, the planet becomes poorer: because to make any type of product, a natural resource or human resource somewhere on the planet must become impoverished. By purchasing more products than we need, we are boosting the oligarchs who control the production of goods, while actively encouraging further natural destruction. Our civilization is ecologically corrupt.

Each consumer product is another distraction. Each transaction is another monetization of our unhappiness. The Unhappiness Machine may have helped capitalism, but it has presented a lose-lose situation for humans, even for those in power: it gave people the illusion of happiness, while ripping them apart forever from the free, simple, and less stressful things that used to make them genuinely, truly happy. In our obsession to service the Machine, we have become too busy, too self-absorbed to even notice, recognize, admire and enjoy the beauty of this planet. Surely if we cannot appreciate beauty we must be at the most dangerous point in our history. If we can't admire beauty, then we won't protect it.

We are the only species on Earth who has willingly settled for living in polluted environments toxic to its physical and mental health. Our civilization doesn't just cause ecological collapse, it actually embodies it.

In order to serve the Unhappiness Machine, people had to become machines as well. Our work culture treats humans like machines with a predefined working lifetime, expiration date and baseline expected performance. We are often made to feel guilty when sick, and considered a liability to the stability of the overall system, rather than as biological organisms who should be entitled to their good days, and their not-so-good days. We should be organisms entitled to their own life and death on our own terms. From bullying to burnout, our economic system relies on doing to workers what it has done to nature for hundreds of years. This culture of exploitation is what has brought this planet's climate to its knees.

Humans may have abolished racial slavery within their species, but hundreds of forms of slavery continue to be the fundamental driving force behind our global economic system. Modern humans have been forced into the "work, sleep, repeat" pattern to cater to capitalism's "produce, sell, repeat". We all serve the insatiable capitalist CO_2 machine, risking our health and freedom in order to make others rich. Our ability to scale up production and obliterate entire ecosystems in the process, depends on keeping this planet and the 8 million species that live on it enslaved. We have put shackles on every single resource that exists on this planet, exploiting it to death. Every single one of us is a slave master and slave at the same time, simply by association with this toxic economic system that relies on exploitation for its very survival. Despite collectively dominating over the planet, humans are arguably the most oppressed, repressed and exploited species. Those who play by the rules of the system become rewarded and promoted to "superslaves". Corporations have evolved sophisticated cultures and processes that reward the most selfish, ignorant and morally corrupt employees. Then these "high achievers" become leaders who, ironically, promise to fight selfishness, ignorance and lack of compassion. If a system continues to allow leaders with no ethics or honesty to survive, then it is not the leader that's the problem. It is the corrupt system and our personal corruption, both on a personal and collective level.

There are no corrupt politicians. There are corrupt political ecosystems which select for them, endorse them, promote them and maintain them in power.

Crucial to this transformation of human beings into machines was the development of city life and the development of Urban Sadness, which became additional food for the Unhappiness Machine. Cities became places where the incomes of ordinary people were robbed, and consumption was boosted by a deep sense of unfulfillment that the city tried to instill into all its inhabitants. Yet another trap that capitalism set for humans was the invention of "income": unlike genuine life experiences, income is never enough, it isn't actually meaningful, and never results in true happiness. Everyone had to have ambitious career goals, and everyone had to feel ashamed of how they live in comparison to a rich neighbor. As the cost of urban living went up, peoples' mental health went down. They began chasing after money and "things", living robotic lives paycheck to paycheck, working not to better their lives anymore, but to simply pay their rent. Their life's purpose became to serve The Machine.

The rent slaves of the city eventually became unhappy because their lives lacked genuine meaning. Even the city's mass-manufactured products and entertainment were not enough to lift them out of their depression. Most of the products didn't really fulfil any tangible, urgent needs. They were there merely for the purpose of robbing people of their income, and to leave them feeling even more empty so that they come back and purchase more useless products, just in case these new products "worked better" and perhaps would finally make them happy.

All of those free, fun activities that people used to do in the countryside were now long forgotten in the city. They had been replaced by expensive, artificial, ready-made, pre-planned and pre-booked entertainment. And this was by far the biggest heist in the history of human civilization: robbing people of the genuine meaning their lives used to have, robbing them of their right to live simply, right here, right now, and be genuinely happy simply by existing. The cage of the big city robbed people of the choice to live how they wanted. You could say that, it robbed them of their consciousness.

Capitalism converted our former meaningful existence to a cold transaction. Nothing feels real anymore, because nothing is genuinely meaningful. Even the sixth mass extinction is a business venture, instead of a holocaust. Capitalism introduced us to millions of products, addictions and preoccupations. These in fact became millions of ways to feel even more unsatisfied, incomplete, confused, empty and unhappy. We are so addicted to these distractions that they have become coping mechanisms: the closer collapse approaches, the more distractions people have at their disposal to keep them busy while they wait for the lights of civilization to switch off.

The biggest irony of the collapse which our civilization is currently undergoing is that, as electricity, supply chains and technology eventually begin to lessen their stranglehold on our lives, many people will actually feel happier, even though life will be much tougher.

THE PARADOX OF INNOVATION

Civilizations always experience sudden, breakneck-speed growth when they encounter innovation. Fire, metalworking, intensive agriculture, electricity, money, transportation, a regulated workforce and so on, have all in turn, completely transformed what used to be a species of nomadic foragers. While these indeed are "innovations" when they first emerge, they soon become integrated into the bedrock of the civilization much like the gears and hydraulics in a car: invisible from the outside, but vital to its daily function. At one point simply "good to have", now they have become integrated into the bedrock of the civilisation in a symbiotic relationship: the innovations need the civilisation to exist, and the civilisation simply cannot carry on without them. It has become hostage to the innovations it invented, almost like an organism giving birth to its own parasite.

With each stage of civilizational development, the list of innovations that are part of this essential bedrock becomes longer. Each era brings its own innovations, which depend on all previous innovations e.g. internet depends on electricity, electricity depends on fire and fossil fuels. As a result, the list of essential components that each successive civilization needs to simply function daily becomes longer and longer. What started as a simple wheelbarrow, is now a super-expensive car consisting of thousands of parts.

The issue is that it is much easier to maintain and repair a wheelbarrow than a Rolls Royce. The very manufacture and existence of a Rolls Royce depends on the health of an entire economic and political machine: the supply chains for the import of foreign-made parts, mining companies that supply the rare earth minerals, labor unions that protect the employees, universities that churn out engineers, politicians that endorse big manufacturing investments.

Three decades ago, we could still imagine a world without e-mail. Today we wouldn't even know where to begin in imagining such a world. This demonstrates the paradox of innovation: although innovations bring about capabilities and advancements, they hold civilizations hostage to their own success: once you have electricity, there is no option ever to go powerless again, unless the entire society collapses. Today, internet is just as important as fire was to early humans.

Each innovation is in fact another Achilles' Heel for the civilisation. Like the algae living inside a coral, innovations are sensitive to perturbations. They are not only useless without the environment that the civilisation provides for them, but they depend on a fragile, intricate web of other, equally fragile innovations. In fact, an innovation is rarely ever a genuine game-changer. It is usually a mere improvement, often the result of a synergy between two or more facets of technology that already existed.

Since they are built upon each other in this way like a house of cards, all innovations form a fragile interdependency web. Failure in one can bring failure in all others. And while the interdependency web itself forms to create synergies between the innovations, this works in reverse when just one of the innovations suddenly fails. Whether it is a supply chain, or the supply of electricity to various appliances, failure in one can mean failure in all.

What is interesting is that the civilization is always caught by surprise. The downward spiral comes out of nowhere, for the simple reason that the civilization had underestimated the incredible co-dependency between the innovations – and taken for granted the innovations themselves in the first place.

For example, there will never be an emergency plan in place for the world running out of energy or internet. Just like climate change, this scenario is existentially, politically, and socially impossible to even imagine.

Yet it doesn't mean that it is not likely. The truth is that civilizations never learn from their mistakes. Rather, they repeat them using updated technologies, hoping that the outcome will be different this time around.

Our media systems also evolve and "innovate" in order to maintain social cohesion and faith towards the system: myths are constantly woven around the infallibility and resilience of our innovations. These myths rely on other myths, and so on and so forth, creating an interdependency web of myths, also known as culture, which is similar to the web of innovations. Innovations tend to be put on a pedestal without exception, becoming part of the essential fabric and identity of society, like religions that are never to be questioned. They become part of our "mission", whether it is to conquer other planets or become God himself.

Yet it is not these innovations that will be the highlight of our "Curriculum Vitae". All the triumphs, discoveries, innovations and other milestones of the human race's brief presence on Earth will only be fine print on our final legacy. Our greatest achievement, putting much of the planet's ecosystems permanently out of existence, will trump all previous achievements and milestones over the duration of our short-lived civilization. Planetary destruction will become our greatest legacy: trumping every major discovery, every painting or sculpture, every musical masterpiece conceived. We will finally find our elusive purpose. It will give a dark, stark and surprising answer to the question we have been asking ourselves all along:

"Who are we? Where do we come from? Where are we going?"

In our pointless obsession to have a "purpose" and a "mission" on a planet where all other species are happy to just exist, we will have finally gotten what we wanted, and "left our mark". The purpose, the mission we have been looking for in these few thousand years is now finally clear, and it wasn't at all what we had imagined. The butterfly has suddenly woken up and realized it's a mosquito. Whichever way one spins it, planetary destruction cannot qualify as either an achievement or a mission. It is simply the accidental, blind side effect of arrogance and gluttony.

Our new "emperors" are techno-narcissists the likes of Elon Musk and Mark Zuckerberg who pretend to know about innovation, physics and technology, but conveniently forget that stupidity is thermodynamically impossible. No space rocket or Metaverse will ever refreeze a melted arctic, revive a rainforest, or jump start the Gulf Stream.

The planet, and humanity, are being destroyed by innovation and capitalism. They are being destroyed by something that is not even another biological entity or life form. But it is almost sentient, as it is able to speak to us, manipulate us. We have created a monster made of algorithms. As greed becomes digital and profit maximization is driven by AI, the hungry beast is speeding up. The worst is yet to come. These new "beings" can't feel emotions or appreciate biological life. They are made to be "efficient", like any war machine. We live in a world where equality, environment and life forms that "get in the way" are indiscriminately sacrificed in order to optimise for efficiency, effectiveness and profit. This civilisation is doomed.

When a civilization dies due to a sudden fault in one or more of its innovations, with it dies any memory or retrospective perspective over what led to the collapse. The erroneous conclusion is often that the cause wasn't the haphazard, fragile web of innovations and supply chains, but extraordinary "outside" events. The cycle begins again, with the next civilization making the same mistakes, inventing its own long list of innovations. Its own long list of Achilles' Heels.

THE CURSE OF THE SELF-DESTRUCTIVE PREDATOR

Every ecosystem takes steps to curb species that over-proliferate. Those with long arms who continuously eat more than their fair share are always brought to justice and pay a hefty population price. As the population of the species explodes, alarms go off. The ecosystem senses a bottleneck in the food chain, an expanding bulge, like a cancer. A mysterious new predator sooner or later appears, able to consume this bulge, unblock the food chain, and allow resources to flow freely again. A heavy cull on the rogue species is inflicted, allowing its molecules to be recycled back into the food chain where they belong.

In fact, each species becomes both predator and prey, so that any bulges or breakages in the food chain are avoided. This system prevents extinctions, as well as the rise of super-predators. It is for this reason that, after 3.8 billion years, 8 million species have evolved on this planet. Earth's ecosystem is the most tolerant, diverse, and egalitarian democracy that we will ever know. All species, however different from each other, share their molecules directly back into the same common nutrient pool, one circular food chain, where all life forms originate, and where they all return to die.

Despite this, humanity has managed to evade the laws of the food chain and climb to a staggering 8 billion-strong population that has already destroyed a large part of the ecosystem. Through its destruction of the climate and habitats, humanity represents an existential threat to the entirety of Earth's ecosystems. We are in fact such a toxic species, that our impact would be felt even long after our disappearance. When most life forms go extinct, they completely surrender their molecules to Earth's nutrient pool. If humans go extinct however, they will leave behind plastic trash and radioactivity. Even if we were to vanish tomorrow, plants would still grow deformed in abandoned nuclear sites. Fish and birds would still be choking on ingested plastic, tens of thousands of years into the future. There is a real possibility that, even if we were to disappear today, we could still be making species extinct well into the future.

Earth has tried many times to cull humanity: be it through viruses, bacteria or other predators it has thrown at us, in the hope that our population would dwindle down to a manageable level that is of little threat to the rest of the food chain. This war continues, and nature is not prepared to surrender its weapons. Even an organism as small as a virus, barely visible to the naked eye and without even a cell membrane, can potentially defeat an advanced civilization. The most lethal, targeted, and devastating biological weapons are not in the hands of humans. They are under Earth's possession, and she will use them whenever and however she sees fit. These weapons are continuously updated in the biggest biological weapons laboratory that exists: Earth's ecosystem.

Nothing stands in the way of an angry, betrayed planet. We are nothing but a house of cards in the wind. Human authority is a myth. The only authority and power on this planet belongs to the forces of nature.

But Earth hasn't even made use of its biggest weapon yet: turning us against ourselves. Humanity is a very special, rare type of super-predator: one that is self-destructive. The more successful a predator is, the more likely that they will go extinct by their own hand. Self-destruction lurks like a chronic disease: fully detectable, yet benign enough to continue its slow advance without raising the alarm. Its power lies not in its intensity, but in its persistence. Self-destruction follows a lazy, incremental progression, building its crescendo under the cover of night. It advances slow enough to fool its victim into believing that there is plenty of time to act, yet never rests: the direction of travel is consistent, and irreversible. By the time "urgent" action is needed, it is already too late.

Self-destruction is almost impossible to stop because it is perpetrated by the self. It is an autoimmune disease where the victim is also the perpetrator. It requires an unusually strong person to stand up to themselves, just like a drug addict whose brain is hijacked by a chemical. In most cases self-destruction continues its dirty work unabated, even as warning signs become starker, louder, impossible to ignore.

Unable to accept that they have lost control, narcissistic predators desperate to save face will embrace their own self-destruction as inevitable. This defeatism brings about a huge emotional relief. Others will choose denial, retreating into a made-up world which they can visit anytime. They will often alternate perpetually between denial and defeatism but will never dare to venture into the realm of fact-checked truth.

Some predators will even claim that they consciously chose their self-destruction, convincing themselves that they are still in control. But they have merely surrendered to the scenario that requires the least amount of effort: death. This morbidly narcissistic, consciously unconscious path to self-destruction brings about a liberating, yet lethal euphoria to the predator. They do indeed feel like they are in control, despite living their most stupid moment. They embrace "living like there is no tomorrow", before realizing that they have denied themselves the chance to live another day.

Humanity's highly addictive, greedy and narcissistic nature

makes it a prime victim of self-destruction, defeatism, and denial. Evolution may not directly select for self-destruction, it does however select for traits that eventually lead to it: greed, intelligence, technological innovation, are the traits that help super predators achieve their meteoric rise to the top – as well as their own self-destruction. We have repeatedly proved that we can solve complex survival problems. Yet by all signs we are incapable of solving our own self destruction. The amount of sacrifice and revolutionary social transformation needed to save this planet from unimaginable tragedy can only become apparent if humanity goes through unimaginable tragedy.

One can argue that self-destruction is our natural fate, and the only long-term option that was ever on the table. If humans were to go back in time, they would have probably done everything the same. Why fix the world when it is much more profitable to smoke it? Why turn down the music when it is more fun to have a loud, raucous party? Humans will do what they have always done, which is to care about their immediate gratification and ignore all other beings, including their own children. We suffer from countless addictions and greed-motivated behaviors that prevent us from assuming the selfless, responsible, compassionate role that we need to play if we are to avert our own destruction. However smart we claim to be, we have failed to achieve escape velocity from greed, narcissism, denial and defeatism.

Hypocrisy is our biggest game. Ethics and ethical dilemmas become important to humans only when convenient: when they serve a specific economic, political or other benefit that caters to one of our many self-destructive addictions. Humanity has always chosen which traffic lights to obey and which to ignore, at will. We are brilliant at inventing myths and religions to justify our actions. If these myths are not convincing enough, we can always resort to defeatism.

In the end, the laws of physics and entropy determine our fate.

Humanity is only a very small part of creation. It can scream and shout, throw tantrums and break things, but ultimately it is the creation that decides where the new balance lies, who stays, and who goes. All predators die when there is no one left to eat. All bullies are powerless when there is no one left to dominate.

THE INEXISTENCE OF
HUMAN SENTIENCE

Although "sentience" is defined as "being able to perceive or feel things", nowadays the term seems to be used exclusively in the context of comparing humans to animals, or to artificial intelligence applications. There is a desperate effort to prove, once and for all, that humans are the only species, or machine for that matter, who can truly "feel" or "perceive". Advocates of such a dogma claim that although animals and some machines can also feel and perceive, we are the only ones who do it with conscious intentionality. In other words, non-human entities are sentient either by accident, or display behaviors that "look" sentient, but aren't. This is human supremacy at its finest, devoid of any supporting proof.

The goal of this of course is to prove that humans belong in a pecking order all on their own. Humans are embarrassed of their natural heritage and association with other life forms on this planet and have always wanted to prove that they are a different class of species altogether, one that is perhaps not ever related to all other life forms, since it is far more superior.

Sentience has always been central to this argument. Not because a more "intelligent" species is necessarily superior, but because advanced intelligence was really the only physical feature that humans could use to support their human supremacy dogma. Other features simply tended to prove the opposite, that we are in fact, quite inferior: we have no hair on our body to protect us from the cold, average eyesight, and inferior sense of smell compared to other animals. Sentience was intentionally "chosen" to support the human supremacy dogma, not because it confers superiority in a species, but because there was little else there to signify that humans were superior. "Sentience" was weaponized by humans to create false narratives about human supremacy, in the same way that skin color was weaponized to create narratives about white supremacy.

Of course, the notion of superiority itself is absurd, and is yet another falsehood that was invented by humans. There are no superior and inferior species on Earth, again because Earth is a cycle, and so is the food chain. All species depend on one another and cannot live without each other, whether they are predators or prey. Furthermore, they are vastly different from each other. Comparing a human to a zebra is comparing apples to oranges. Each one has a completely different role in the ecosystem, there is no superiority/inferiority question.

It is ironic then that the species that by all accounts is "on top" of the ecosystem when it comes to domination and destruction, is the only one preoccupied with the question of superiority, and sentience. If not the most superior or sentient, humans deserve the title of the most insecure of all species. They are the only species who constantly wonders where the hell in the pecking order they belong, because they are also the only species who believes there is such a thing as pecking orders. The other 8 million species of the planet couldn't care less about where their place is. Not because they are less intelligent, but because they are less insecure. They know there are no pecking orders, and that there is an implied order in the ecosystem that presides above it all, as opposed to one species presiding over the rest. No one is ever "on top" in an interdependent, healthy ecosystem. Again, you cannot compare different fruit. In fact, one can argue that it is the single-celled organisms who are on top. Single-celled organisms are the thermostat of this planet. 3.8 billion years ago they created our oxygen-rich atmosphere and pulled CO_2 out of the air as if by magic. Now they are creating the methane bomb that will end humanity and allow Earth to continue. I would say that they are probably at the very top of the pecking order, if such a notion exists.

Humans suffer from perfectionism, which leads to greed, selfishness, jealousy and conflict. Nature is imperfect, yet completely self-sufficient. But it is really deep insecurity that lies at the root of the human supremacy and sentience dogmas. Humans are plagued with insecurity about the future, and about their place in the ecosystem. All other species are more pragmatic, knowing that all that matters is now, and that there is a natural and biological order on the planet that makes any attempts to override it futile. If such a thing as intelligence exists, the ecosystem is really the only brain around, and which follows the laws of physics rather than arbitrary definitions of supremacy. A version of true intelligence that is much less biased and in line with the operating principles of nature then, could be pragmatism: the recognition that everyone and everything on this planet is an important, vital element of the puzzle, however much "sentient" they have been rated out to be by insecure, small-minded humans.

The problem with the concept of "sentience" is that humans have given it an extremely narrow definition, which suits them and only them. All beings on this planet are able to "feel" and "perceive", but they do so in vastly different ways that are simply different from those of humans. A honeybee is able to memorize the location and flowering time of hundreds of flowers and use these two pieces of data to map out the most efficient flight course, a task that would take a human mathematician days to solve. There are many different types of intelligence, and any attempt to arrange species on a pecking order from most to least intelligent will run again and again into the same issue of comparing apples to oranges. Each species has developed its own type of intelligence, simply because it has a different role in the ecosystem.

Hardcore human supremacists will argue that humans are the most sentient as they are the only ones who are "self-aware". But is this a type of intelligence, or is self-awareness a form of insecurity and narcissism? Is awareness of our own death a good thing? It certainly has not helped in preventing homicide and war.

Arguably if we were indeed the most "intelligent", we would also be the most responsible. We wouldn't be pushing other species to extinction and rather than just being "self-aware", we would be most aware than any other species of the value of biological life. Our actions prove the opposite, as we are the most destructive species on the planet. Putting ethics aside, our dark legacy on Earth is strong proof that in fact we have little self-awareness as well as awareness as a whole, and we are unable to learn from our mistakes. Surely this is neither "sentient" or "intelligent".

Any attempt to ever define "sentience" will run into the issue of who is it that is defining it: the humans, the bees, or the dolphins? Each will have their own definition of sentience, and will use its own language to define it, be it words, pheromones or sounds. Even when humans do discover non-human sentience, or even animal languages like the one dolphins speak, they do not consciously try to understand these languages, and simply resort to attempting to translate them into human terminology. Who is to say what is sentient and what isn't when you are using your own subjective "sentience" to attack this question? The entire debate around sentience has taken place strictly within the narrow boundaries of human definitions and constructs, which undoubtedly bias any scientific exploration.

Even serious studies on the intelligence of other species are often biased, looking at intelligence and sentience through the human supremacy lens. These studies are usually looking to detect signs of intelligence skills that humans use in their environment, rather than immersing themselves in the context that a species lives. They also look for memory and brain processing power, rather than intuition or wisdom, which are forms of intelligence more difficult to measure but more universal. We train monkeys to push buttons for food and put octopuses in mazes to see if they are "intelligent", as if intelligence is about overcoming obstacles and collecting strategic military information. We continue to mistake brain power for "intelligence" and "sentience", like the tall kid in the playground who thinks he is stronger than everybody just because he's got a couple of heads over the other kids. So was the octopus that failed to free themselves from a jar really dumb, or could it be that they have been depressed or suicidal and decided to end it all? Are we really listening into the myriad of languages of this planet, or just trying to find echoes of ourselves in other beings?

There are in fact, many arguments against the sentience of humans. Humans are the only species on Earth capable of systematic, methodical, large-scale culling of their own population, often for purely ideological reasons. Humans have the ability to completely detach themselves from any "feeling" or "perceiving" and commit heinous crimes that challenge the imagination, such as the Holocaust or Nuclear War. It is under debate whether these were actions of "sentience", or in fact lack of any form of detectable consciousness whatsoever.

If humans were highly sentient, they would "feel" and "sense" the pull of their umbilical connection to every other life form on Earth, which they literally share the same phylogenetic tree with. Humans have an admirable ability in identifying, analysing and recognising all of the things that they are doing wrong, and yet, carry on doing them anyway. Doing "what is right" is always sacrificed at the altar of greed and narcissism. Compassion and empathy are seen as unexpected, unwanted and unaccounted for overhead expenses within our capitalist system. They are "nice to have", but a threat to the global "economy". Compassion, empathy and emotional intelligence are not really seen as an "intelligent" brain function in our species. Manipulation and calculation, the side-effects of our tremendous brain power, are far more interesting and rewarding, and fit more closely our popularized definition of what "intelligence" is. In fact, "intelligence" today is a synonym for military terminology that means to collect information against the enemy.

Perhaps a more philosophical question which we will never know the answer to is: are species with large brainpower like us always this narcissistic? Do they always have this much "intelligence" but little actual wisdom? If this is true, then the rise of ultra-intelligent species is a death sentence for any planet. The civilizations that any such species creates eventually disable the very ability of a planet to give rise to civilizations. The human type of "sentience" may not be all that it's been hyped up to be.

My penultimate argument against human sentience is that, if indeed sentience was such a "prized" asset, and if humans were the only ones who possessed it, then surely humans would be of immense value to the greater ecosystem of the planet? This is not the case, sadly. Humans are the only one out of 8 million species that offer absolutely nothing to this planet. Not only would Earth not miss humans if they went extinct, our absence would bring instant relief similar to the sudden death of a dictator. The impact would be almost immediate. A species that only exists for itself is a lonely species. Humanity is completely alone, having broken its relationship with all other 8 million life forms of this planet.

It took 3.8 billion years for 8 million species to slowly evolve on Earth. It has taken just a few hundred years for just one of those species to usher in a global ecosystem collapse that will be the biggest extinction event of the planet. The ability of a single species to annihilate an entire "world" of ecosystems seamlessly in balance with each other, will forever remain an unfathomably horrifying holocaust which took place in the only life-rich planet we have ever known. It took place in full awareness of an otherwise "sentient" being that committed this crime. Although we are the only species on the planet that has a religion, we are also the only one who qualifies for hell.

THE ENTERTAINMENT DEATH TRAP

Entertainment is the experience of watching or attending an event, whether real or not, current or past, and relishing the fact that you can be "present" from a safe distance.

The one being entertained usually has an intense curiosity about the subject matter: they want to get as close as they can to "the scene", soak up every fine detail, just like a voyeur. They want to "be there" with all their senses, but not really be there physically, as the latter would come with consequences and complications. They are aroused by the ability to get as close as they like to where the action is, yet be immune to any of the fallout. They would dread becoming a participant in the story, a role which comes with responsibilities, such as having to take decisions that affect the course of events.

Entertainment provides the audience with the best of both worlds: they can have all the fun in the world, but suffer none of the consequences, and own zero of the responsibilities.

It is not difficult to see why this is highly addictive. Entertainment allows the audience to live a "hyper-reality" full of exciting risks and rich scenarios beyond their wildest imagination, even though it is all theatre. This is why some of the most successful entertainment comes in the form of video games, which create this super-exciting hyper-reality that the audience craves. The player feels more alive than ever, living in the shoes of their fearless avatar, an imaginary person that they could never live up to. At the same time, they don't have to endure any of the suffering that their avatar goes through. In fact, as a "player", they have extra lives to spare. They have infinite lives in fact. The ultimate high for the player is that at the end of it all, they get to defeat death (albeit virtually), their worst inner fear.

This is why voyeurism and entertainment are the ultimate highs for humans. The defeat of death, even though virtual, provides a feeling of invincibility, much like Class A drugs. The virtual reality that entertainment provides is addictive, exactly because it is too good to be true. It allows one to safely step out of their comfort zone, without even leaving their armchair. Whatever happens to the avatar can't affect them. If at any point the entertainment isn't fun anymore, they have full control: they can always turn the TV off, switch the channel, start a new video game. The life that you are living as an avatar is the most exciting life you have ever lived, but it is taking place on another universe far away, that can never affect you.

Despite this, the purpose of entertainment has always been to "look and feel as real as possible". This is the paradox, and the attraction at the same time, of living in a simulation. And it hides serious, lethal dangers. The problem is that there are too many real events happening in the world today that are treated as entertainment, because we've played too many video games and seen too much theatre. These real events are glossed over, narrated and passed through the Hollywood filter to such an extent that, even though they are real, they are being processed by the audience as simulations. There are too many real, actual events that are treated by the audience as a simulation, exactly because they have been conditioned to see them as entertainment.

After a while, the voyer becomes unable to distinguish their own life from the hyper-life of their avatar. The lines between reality and hyper-reality begin to blur dangerously. The voyer's addiction to the hyper-reality gets the better of them, as their real life can never measure up to their imaginary world in either vividness, color or intensity. They need a constant supply of their entertainment drugs. And the more they use them, the more unsatisfied they feel with their real life.

As the voyer sinks further and further into hyper-reality, their real, actual life begins to take a turn for the worst, to become neglected. They sink into passive oblivion. They become permanent voyeurs, pursuing escapism and consumerism to the point that entertainment actually does become their real life, at least in their head.

As with all addicts, they become increasingly unable to tend to the everyday things happening right here, right now. They lose any appreciation not only for their own life, but for their family, nature, the small things in life such as two minutes of sunlight or a beautiful flower. The voyer has completely lost track of their real life. All life events are now treated as entertainment: wars, fires, floods are not news to them anymore. They are just images with sound, coming from the video game. In their eyes and ears, these real-life events don't feel real anymore. They have simply become part of the entertainment. They can be safely ignored, just like the events in the life of the avatar.

They are in for a very rude awakening, of course.

It is easy to see how we, as a society, collectively became entertainment zombies. As we began to spend more and more of our lives inside screens, our actual life became part of the entertainment, in the most perverse cognitive inversion that could ever be possible. The worst part of it is that by becoming passive voyeurs, we are unable to see, critique and manage our own reality. We can only live inside the video game, which has been carefully manicured by corporations, governments and elites who want us to progress from one level of the game to the next in predictable, controlled, pre-determined steps without questioning who we are, where we are, and where we are going.

We are in fact, not even real anymore. We have become the

avatar. We have become digital code. As substance and humanity gradually disappear from civilization, so do the common sense and critical thinking which are so essential in processing and critiquing our reality.

Death arrives suddenly, as the voyer realizes too late that this was not in fact a video game. There is no START NEW GAME screen. The real game, which is the game of all games, is now over.

THE LIE OF CLEAN ENERGY

While nature gradually goes dark during the winter months, and plants and animals decrease their metabolic activity almost down to zero, there is one species that represents a bizarre aberration to the planet's seasonal metabolic patterns. Humans continue to consume throughout the winter, their energy use increasing while most other species go into hibernation.

Dependent on their electric lights, gas heating and automobiles, humans represent an immense anomaly in the natural energy grid of the planet. This energy grid was once limited to sunlight, chemical energy from food, and geothermal sources. By unearthing fossil fuels and harnessing electrical energy, humans have not only expanded this grid for their own selfish use but decimated the planet in the process.

Our civilization has always focused on "harnessing" energy rather than managing energy use, the assumption always being that energy and other resources are infinite; therefore, if there is a lack, we should simply harness more energy rather than manage what we are using. This belief became yet another important foundational "truth" in our civilization's exponential expansionist model. A "no limits" policy on energy and water use still exists throughout humanity. The more the better, and any increase in demand is a legitimate reason for an increase in natural destruction to achieve the new energy quotas. We still believe that there are no limits: the more energy, the better. Whether it is fossil fuel or food, humans stash away as much energy as they can. And while everyone wants to have more of it, no one ever knows how to spend it wisely.

This foundational belief is also the reason why sustainable development has not focused on managing energy consumption, but on further ramping up energy production. The doctrine that energy production can be ramped up in a sustainable manner is a capitalist myth and an oxymoron, because "sustainable" energy is a myth all to itself. Wind turbines and electric vehicle batteries barely ever compensate for the carbon footprint of their construction, transport and operation by the time they have reached the end of their lifetime and become useless, toxic landfill waste.

We need solutions to manage our energy use, not to service its exponential increase. By continuing this path all we are servicing is natural destruction and inequality. As long as we have an insatiable need for energy and an unwavering crave for the latest fashion, there will be petrochemical oligarchs and sweatshops. There will be climate breakdown and extinction.

"Green energy" is the biggest successful re-brand ever perpetrated. An entire for-profit industry successfully convinced consumers that it had "cleansed itself", when in fact it merely updated its technological approach to natural destruction.

The "renewable energy industrial complex", aka the fossil fuel industry, has not changed. It still relies on an economic growth model of increasing demand, rather than finding ways to downsize our demand. It still focuses on how it can service this increasing energy demand and make money for its investors. What the renewable energy industrial complex ignores is that making our energy renewable is not a technology issue, but a social issue. It is about changing our lifestyle, not producing more energy from sources that are anything but "green".

But social issues are the first issues governments run away from. Our society has already proved that it would rather create mini suns in mega particle colliders, than fully use the energy of the one, real sun that is already there, and which is more than enough for all of us. It has proved that it would rather pursue the holy grail of developing carbon capture technology, when there is one already in existence in the form of trees. The renewable energy industrial complex wants to have its cake and eat it too. We are constantly fed myths about how renewable energy will allow us to continue to ramp up our energy use with the aid of powerful renewable energy, as if the production of solar panels and EV batteries has no impact or carbon footprint.

The truth is that the concepts of "renewable" energy and "sustainability" were corrupted and weaponized almost at their inception, and before they could even take hold. Sustainability became the art of deluding consumers into buying products that magically de-consume themselves. Greenwashed renewable energy investments became nothing but a shopfront for environmental crime, and a hopeless cat and mouse game kicked off between "green" technology and regulation, whereby the renewable industrial complex is allowed to destroy Earth faster than any new environmental legislation can catch up. Almost every product now has its "green alternative": its more "presentable sister", who however is just as sinister and just as destructive on the inside.

We are more preoccupied with the ephemeral construction of the edifices that our civilization produces, rather than their re-cyclability and re-usability. It is profoundly ironic that humans have put so much effort in creating two materials that will last forever i.e. plastics and radioactivity, yet themselves they have become an evolutionary dead end. Even if humans went extinct, under ideal conditions much of the plastic they left behind wouldn't decompose until at least 1,000 years into the future. The Anthropocene would be followed by the silent millennium of the Plasticene.

All "sustainable" solutions marketed by politicians and

corporations come from people like you and I who just needed a job: they were once hired as consultants to work for a company and paid salaries to develop "renewable" technologies, for the ultimate purpose of winning contracts, earning investments, selling products, and making a profit for their stakeholders. Inherrently profit-motivated and human-centered, sustainability is an oxymoron and will never be "sustainable", simply because nature was never included in the long list of stakeholders.

In fact, the majority of humanity itself is usually not included in the stakeholders list either. Profit, capitalism and consumption benefited only segments of human society throughout our history, and have always, without exception, destroyed Earth in the process. All that remains after the destruction is stale greenwashing propaganda created by marketers and PR gurus living in their own sustainability delusion bubbles, spending their time managing perceptions and magically turning brown to green. They become self-proclaimed "Earth defenders". But Earth is not waiting to be "saved" by anyone. Earth is waiting to be left alone.

The reality is that, in order to manufacture anything "sustainable" or "clean", you always have to pollute something else. At the heart of this is the human model of manufacturing and economic growth itself, which puts profit before purpose. Manufacturing and economic growth are both dirty processes because they are based on depletion and exploitation, as this is the production model that results in maximum profit. Almost everything that humans have created during their brief history on this planet had to involve some element of natural destruction. Meanwhile human rights and the protection of the environment are, and have always been, the biggest impediments to profit.

Both primitive and modern humans suffered from the same, infinite delusion that they can continue to deplete and exploit until the end of time. They both failed to realise that the day we ceased to have natural predators, was the day we became responsible for controlling our own population size. Thanks to capitalism and the industrial revolution, the cheap mass production of goods resulted in the cheap mass production of more humans. 150 species are made forever extinct each day, just as 385,000 additional human babies are born into a world of diminishing resources. That's 2,500 more humans per day per extinct species. We are replacing the Creation with copies of ourselves. Every new baby brought into this collapsing world not only constitutes child abuse, it is also a CO_2 mega bomb that by far dwarfs the carbon footprint of any other single human activity on the planet. We are literally the weeds in an overgrown Garden of Eden, the algae that is suffocating the river of life. And that, is definitely not sustainable.

THE TRAVESTY OF GOVERNMENT

There was a time when many people believed that Governments were the ultimate safety net. Many of us, including myself, believed that, despite all their faults and inefficiencies, governments, at least the so-called "democratic" ones, were better than no government at all. We believed that the government was a place where big, important, and intelligent brains, at least for most of the time, took responsible decisions. Sometimes they got it wrong, but in general, their intention was to strive for the "common good" and ensure that humanity will continue, in some form or other.

But the phrase "death by committee" wasn't coined for nothing. Today, failed COP after failed COP meeting has proved exactly this: that our governments are driving us to our own death. It is a mass collective suicide decided at the supra-governmental, planetary level.

The reason is simple: collective decision-making is an oxymoron. Because we are not living in a democracy, but a collection of puppet governments enslaved to Business as Usual. Each of the puppets is given an equal right to vote, so while in technical terms there is an illusion of democracy, in real terms every single individual vote is rigged. Trying to achieve meaningful consensus under these circumstances is not only unrealistic and overly ambitious, but also pointless, considering that everyone is effectively corrupt. At best, what is achieved is a complete decision deadlock, which however is carefully word-smithed and media-spinned to look as if a triumphant agreement has been reached. Our governments are about to kill us all, but before you start blaming "elites", politicians, and governments, have a think about your own role in this. Put yourself in the shoes of an elected senior decision maker. Choosing what is "good for the planet" would require each of these stakeholders to come into direct conflict with their "stake": the oligarchs, corporations, and political polls that they are hostage to, and which in fact they owe their own rise to power to. They need to always balance what is "good" for justice and for the planet with the interests of corporate greed. Even the most "ethical" politician cannot work in their own ethical vacuum. They all have strings, like the puppets that they are, and must work within the corrupt system that they are part of.

Even when an "ethical decision" is reached, this is not the result of meaningful debate or ethical responsibility, but of a complex, careful rebalancing of all the puppet strings: each new law is nothing but a slightly different configuration of the puppet's posture. The actual result of political "consensus" is usually a meaningless, fragile "pact" that can break down at any moment, if just one of the strings suddenly starts pulling more than the others.

What we perceive as "democracy" then, is just the collective balancing of all mutual "strings" and exploitation relationships within society. And this is really what has always been the role of government: not to do "good things" for humans and the planet, but to keep all the corruption, exploitation and aggression from getting out of control, by establishing some additional puppet strings i.e. rules and regulations.

These mutual strings of exploitation and laws superimposed on them keep the puppet of society standing, preventing major conflict, but that doesn't mean that all the ugliness and evil actors are not there. The outside picture may look stable and orderly, but each of the puppet's strings wants to have its own way. Underneath the static picture of a perfectly composed puppet, lies a vastness of animalistic power relationships that are kept in check through laws, guns, physical borders, threats, social castes, and money. These are the strings that keep it all "together", and the role of government is to oversee all this.

We live under the illusion of "democracy" as a system that creates good in the world, but it doesn't, because democracy relies on government. Democracy is a system more concerned with equality between puppet votes, rather than with the validity, quality and freedom of each individual vote. Yet so many of us still believe that "saving the planet" is possible within the current systems of economic and political governance, even though these systems are increasingly proving themselves to be nothing but planetary suicide machines.

But as much as these politicians and "systems" are to blame, so are we, the so-called "ordinary citizens". We invented democracy with the pretense of being able to voice our opinion, yet we overindulge in delegating this opinion, and the tough job of governance, to someone else who "represents" us: a high-ranking individual who we can hold responsible and pass the blame to for all the problems we cannot solve.

But these high-ranking individuals have already called our bluff, and they can play this game equally well. So instead of stressing about their responsibility as leaders, they simply let us down, passing the responsibility back to us. An endless ping-pong process is about to begin.

After all, leaders are humans themselves, not superheroes. And they certainly do not want to break any of their strings, becoming martyrs for "choosing the righteous path". They will avoid controversial decisions at any cost, just like we avoid becoming involved in politics, switching off lights in the house or reducing our fossil fuel footprint. Today's politicians mirror today's humans: they lack all of the qualities that our economic system has successfully exterminated: empathy, critical thinking, and above all, a conscience.

As we, the "ordinary citizens", continue to play along with the democratic illusion, so do the politicians. Both sides are pretending to not know what's going on and continue the ping pong game. But in the end, we all become puppets of our sinful ignorance. We sink into denial, convincing ourselves that at least some of these senior decision makers may do the right thing and suffer for our own sins. Occasionally a few politicians spring up who pretend that they are outsiders, and rise to fame by attacking the hypocrisy of the system. But all they are is good actors. Many of us will vote for these fascists, but they are no different. We are yet again placing our hope and trust in governments and politicians. The more they pretend, the more we pretend that we don't know they are pretending.

The illusion of democracy, and the ping pong game between voters and politicians, are deeply rooted in our cultures. We build houses of parliament, senates and capitol hills. We create stories and textbooks that idealize power and authority, and only rarely do we rebel against them. The boring, pantomime choreography of mirrored movements between the voter and politician continues, as one passes the hot potato back to the other. The show ends, the curtain falls, and both voters and politicians clap for themselves. They clap so hard, that they cannot hear the implosion of civilization.

THE FASCISM OF THE HUMAN SUPREMACY BUBBLE

The invention of the concept of entitlement is yet another example of the futile attempts of our species to rewrite nature's laws. By proclaiming ourselves "entitled" to resources like food and water, we have sought to convince ourselves that we actually "own" these resources, in unlimited quantities.

Ownership, and the many entitlements that we have enshrined into what we call "law", are inventions of the human imagination's wishful thinking. They only exist within the context of human culture because they simply do not compute within the physical laws of the planet. Earth is a cyclical closed system, meaning that nothing can ever be "owned". Ownership is, at best, fleeting and temporary - passed on or inherited from one species to the next. Any aspiration beyond this is blasphemy. All resources on Earth are shared and recycled, just like all matter. On Earth there is no yours or mine. We are all molecules, converting into each other. Outside of the context of human society and culture, ownership is an absurd concept that doesn't exist.

It is true that all species claim things for themselves though. They all feel that they "deserve" to have "things", especially in the various niches they occupy and where they try to establish territorial "rights". However, humans are the only species who has developed an ideological framework to support their claim to territory and resources. The basis of this ideological framework is the most fascist, totalitarian, and narcissistic dogma about how this democracy of 8 million species we call Earth should be run. Humans believe that they deserve resources not because they are hungry, but because they are supreme and superior beings that preside over the ecosystem, much like gravity and energy. They believe that they should have first access to all that the planet has to offer, simply because they are human. Like monarchs, or white supremacists, humans are the only species that feel entitled, simply by virtue of the blue blood that runs through their veins. If slavery is a concept born out of white supremacy, then ownership is a man-invented concept born out of human supremacy. Ownership, and money, are the operating principles of human society.

Of course, the rest of the planet does not operate in this way. Food and other resources are freely allocated to the 8 million species of this planet following the laws of competition and pure chance, and this is how Earth has managed to develop such rich, complex, and diverse ecosystems. Nature does not favor one species over another through rights and privileges, giving every single one the chance to thrive. However much "special" or "entitled" humans themselves may feel, they do not get preferential treatment. Entitlement, ownership, supremacy, and superiority are artificial labels which humans have awarded themselves, and which are toxic to all biological life, including human life.

Sharing of food, water, space is the only way to run such a complex system as Earth. The principle of sharing ensures that everyone has something to live on, even during tough times. Everyone gets an equal share of the surplus when times are good and there is extra food and water to go around, and likewise, the pain is equally distributed among species when times are hard, and resources are low.

Earth's ecosystem is a socialist one, whereby everyone is a stakeholder: everyone has something to gain and something to win, but never at the expense of others. The success of Earth's ecosystems lies precisely on the concept of sharing resources, which keeps all species in balanced competition with each other.

This balanced competition in turn ensures the survival of each species no matter what, and is responsible for the tremendous biodiversity on this planet which peaked a few thousand years ago before humans began to decimate Earth.

Ownership is autocratic. It is a declaration of war to the 8 million species of the planet. A land and resource grab at the other species' expense, even if this means their immediate extinction. The false narrative of human supremacy is a foundation of all civilizations, enshrined through "Human Rights" and "laws" more concerned with how resources are distributed between humans, rather than with the fact that all of these resources are stolen in the first place.

A "human right" therefore, although considered sacred within the confines of human society, is actually a fascist term in the planetary context. Human rights and entitlements infringe on the very existence of all other non-human species, which have no such "rights" simply because they were not born human. The absurdity is only evident if one steps outside of the human supremacy bubble all of us have been nurtured in. Outside of this bubble, human rights are illogical constructs conceived once upon a time by a narcissistic species that was so insecure about "possessions", it refused to share the planet with other life forms. It invented ownership and divided everything into "yours" and "mine" – not in order to establish "rights", but to secure privileges that they were never entitled to in the first place.

Laws and the legal profession were built around this manufactured narrative of "rights" which only exists within the human supremacy bubble. The absurdity of laws is that they apply only to humans. Everyone is equal against the law if they are human, much like all Athenians in classical Greece had equal voting rights, as long as they were neither women or slaves. At best, Earth is a democracy of a single species, with 8 million other species reduced to helpless spectators, excluded from participation in this corrupt political system.

As the list of "rights" and "laws" became longer and more elaborate, the human species eventually got together and awarded itself a long, long list of privileges: More than 193 countries ratified the Declaration of Human Rights, which safeguards the right to food, housing, education, health and stipulates that all individuals belonging to the human species, and only that species, should be treated equally: with fairness, dignity and respect.

Of course, given that the Human Rights Act was conceived, written, decided upon, and voted in by humans only, it tends to be a bit biased. All other 8 million species have no right to a habitat that they can call home. No right to a food source that won't be depleted by humans. No right to their safety and well-being, not even the right to exist, and continue as a species on Earth. Our entire civilization is a fascist regime. Making another species extinct is the most extreme form of violence and fascism that exists. It is the permanent, irrecoverable deletion of a species from the present, future, and even the past. We are a very long way from genuinely accepting, embracing and protecting diversity, biodiversity and difference both within our own species and outside of it.

Before industrial humans came along, Earth was a thriving democracy of 8.7 million species finding strength and mutual support in their diversity. It is now a capitalist dictatorship, pushing its citizens to extinction at an alarmingly accelerating rate. Every species on this planet is a slave, working for humans in some form or other. Imagine if the Amazon rainforest was to go on strike. The slave masters would soon run out of oxygen.

Unfortunately, Earth does not know how to be selfish. Nevertheless, it has the power to rebalance itself since its ecosystems follow the only real "laws" and "rights" that exist: those of physics. Selfish, independent actors that want everything for themselves are eventually sussed out by the ecosystem and punished handsomely. Our planet may not know what selfishness, entitlement and ownership are, but it has its eyes and ears out, and it has already decided: "The Human Rights Act is the epitome of the supremacy bubble. It is the legitimization of the tyranny of humans on Earth. These are not human rights. These are human crimes."

THE FRAUD OF SATAN CLAUS

Santa is a great salesman. He is a public relations spokesman for capitalism, and the first politician and influencer that human children are exposed to when they grow up. This is the critical age when all children learn the very important message: "only through presents and products can a human being ever be truly happy".

By contrast, children that do not get presents are unhappy children, even though they may have loving parents. If a child has no presents, it was either a bad child, or had bad parents. Santa Claus teaches us the very important learning that without presents, there is no love.

Santa is very friendly and will have many product recommendations for you, but you have to understand that he is one busy man. He doesn't get on his reindeer sleigh for nothing. There is commission to be made, which comes from Santa's main employer, Amazon. He pretends to share this commission with his elves: made-up creatures which are as fake as Santa himself.

The real elves are actually humans that reside over in Asia, where they are busy round the clock making toys. Many of Santa's real elves are actually children. These are the bad children that did not deserve toys, but instead have to make toys for the good children, with very little salary and terrible working conditions.

Santa doesn't have reindeer anymore, ever since they became an endangered species. Instead, the toys are put on big supertanker container ships that run on fossil fuel. By the time they have reached their destination, the toys have amassed so much carbon footprint and violated so many animal and human rights, but this is unfortunately the price we must all pay for love. It is all worth it, as at least some of the children on Earth get to have presents.

The bad children are also sometimes lucky. This is because the good children throw away most of their presents, which are then shipped to third world countries as garbage. There, the bad children can walk through burning mountains of garbage and occasionally find a good toy. They must be careful though, not to breathe in the carcinogenic fumes as they will die before they reach adulthood.

Eventually there are too many fumes, and both the good and the bad children breathe them in, as well as the next generation of children.

But love is still there, and so are the toy sweatshops, and most importantly, Santa Claus gets to keep his job.

THE ILLUSION OF HOPE

No human civilization has ever consciously, successfully limited its net negative impact on the planet's species and resources. Never, ever in our history, has our impact on the planet diminished, except perhaps during events out of our control or conscious intention: plagues, wars and similar situations which resulted in either a big economic recession or a decrease in global human population. Every time these events occurred, Earth breathed a brief sigh of relief.

Given that we've never succeeded then, why is it that so many humans still believe that "something" can be done to save Earth? Isn't it strange that the species responsible for the destruction of Earth is also the one seriously contemplating how it can "save" it? Would you trust that species to find a "solution"? It seems that we have an issue here. The real problem is not saving the planet, but what to do about the species that is destroying it. The climate Armageddon is a human-induced Holocaust wiping out billions of life forms on Earth. The scale of this crime is as unfathomable as the scale of our arrogance. Many of those who still hope that "we", the humans, can save the planet, are forgetting that we are the perpetrators. In order to save Earth from the climate apocalypse and ecological holocaust, we would first have to completely reinvent humanity. We are unfortunately arrogant enough to think that this is feasible by signing a few papers at those COP conventions where delegates from all over the world fly in on fossil-fueled planes just to have some croissants.

The summation of humanity's arrogance and denial can be condensed in one word: "Hope". The empty basket of hope is where our imploding, collapsing civilization has now placed all of its eggs. Not a smart, or rational choice, but a justified one. Only through false hope can the current capitalist system have a full license to continue to operate, to continue to destroy what is left of this planet. Hope is an important ingredient not in safeguarding the planet's future, but in keeping the ridiculous game of charades going for just a little bit longer in the present. Hope is not about changing things or having a revolutionary vision, no; hope is about changing absolutely nothing and maintaining the current status quo and business as usual.

Hope is not what it seems. Hope is destructive. Hope is the opposite of pragmatism. Hope does not energise people. It makes them complacent. It makes them oblivious to the dark reality of how toxic all human civilisations have been to this planet. Hope is the ultimate gaslighting. Hope is telling the patient that they are not walking towards their death, but that they are taking a walk in the park in amongst the roses. Hope is equal to blindness. Hope is fucking bullshit.

If the current civilization ever had a sliver of a chance of surviving in the future in some form or other rather than spectacularly imploding, it would be if the planet's survival was put first, and on equal par with the survival of the civilisation. And this can only happen if our civilisation looks around and surveys the desperation and hopelessness of mass extinction that humans have caused on Earth already. Human civilisation is a nightmare within a nightmare. The more you wake up to the reality of how we've put this house of cards together, the more you feel like screaming. This is the natural, healthy reaction to the monstrosity that have created on Earth. But it will only happen if the embarrassing delusion of hope stops at this minute. It will only happen if this civilisation wakes up from the hopium coma, looks through the fumes and realizes that nearly 40% of Earth's land surface is subjugated to agriculture. We live on a dystopian planet where the harvesting robots are constantly going up and down fields of monoculture crops, killing the planet's carbon sinks, its climate machine and its biodiversity. But this is also an intelligent planet: one that watches what we do, and updates its software accordingly. Those who fail to acknowledge the intelligence and wisdom of this planet sooner or later come face to face with it.

Doomers are often accused of hopelessness and pessimism. But I do have a lot of hope. I hope for a world almost devoid of humans, where a somewhat rich biodiversity can begin to thrive again. We could have still been a thriving civilization at much lower population numbers, but we just couldn't settle for less. Our exponential trajectory on this planet leaves no room for doubt: we will be coming very close to the edge of extinction.

BOOKS BY THIS AUTHOR

Pocket Philosophy For End Times

Disposable Earth

A New Earth

Manufactured by Amazon.ca
Bolton, ON

34997102R00049